Grzegorz Marciniak

Protection of the image as a personal right on social networks

Grzegorz Marciniak

Protection of the image as a personal right on social networks

Protection of the image on social media in Polish law

Wydawnictwo Bezkresy Wiedzy

Imprint

Cover image: www.ingimage.com

Publisher:
Editorial Académica Española
is a trademark of
International Book Market Service Ltd., member of OmniScriptum Publishing Group
17 Meldrum Street, Beau Bassin 71504, Mauritius

Printed at: see last page
ISBN: 978-620-2-44607-5

Grzegorz Marciniak

PROTECTION OF THE IMAGE AS A PERSONAL RIGHT *IN VIVO* AND *POST MORTEM* ON SOCIAL NETWORKS IN POLISH LAW

legal status as at 31/05/2017

Non omnis moriar

Horacy

+ Marek Marciniak- Beloved Dad, Officer of the Polish Army.
Memory will not disappear even after years,
because it will be preserved in memories and children's works ...

SUMMARY

PROTECTION OF THE IMAGE AS A PERSONAL RIGHT *IN VIVO* AND *POST MORTEM* ON SOCIAL NETWORKS

Presenting issues of the protection of the image is a purpose of this work as in vivo personal rights of the man and the fast mortem on community portals. The study consists of three chapters. In first from them, the author showed the definition of the image attempts, legal protection of the image ensured in the civil code and in the act on the copyright and related rights.

The chapter two is discussing infringements and the protection of the image of users of community portals. Analysis of the case law of verdicts of Polish courts which constitute the specific interpretation of provisions of the substantive law was described. Notions were moved closer from a point of view of Internet users and the most important statements applying to the protection of their image online.

In the third chapter the infringements concerning the protection of the image are a subject of deliberations on portals of community persons of the deceaseds. An attempt to characterize the being of personal rights was made fast mortem and a concept was shown their protections in doctrine.

At the work comments were used for provisions of the civil code, monographs and articles, also of author of the work which became a cause of an interest in examined issues. Also a judicial decision of courts of general jurisdiction was being indicated in a wide range. In the study a legal-dogmatic method was used.

Key words: civil law, act on the copyright, personal rights, image

TABLE OF CONTENTS

ADMISSION

Social networks process personal data of millions of people, millions of photos are made available almost every second. The danger of violating personal rights is therefore very high. Personal goods such as: identity, personal dignity, pseudonym or image are particularly exposed. Do legal provisions aimed at protecting these goods keep pace with the development of new information and communication technologies?

Legal protection of the image is undoubtedly an important issue nowadays. Creating and sharing an image is very easy nowadays. Of course, information technologies and communication technologies are constantly improving. The development of mobile telephony, IT progress, the Internet make it possible to record the image in almost all circumstances and - without a problem within dozens of seconds - making it available to a wide group of recipients.

The aim of this work is to analyze legal norms regarding the protection of the image of users on social networks, as well as the indication of violations and the possibility of protecting the image of the deceased.

The basis for the research is the hypothesis: do regulations contained in Polish law adequately protect the image of man in vivo and post mortem on social networks?

Protecting the image on social networks is connected with the solution of many dilemmas, and this study is the voice in the discussion on the functioning of image protection in practice. The author of the study gave a lecture on the same title during the National Scientific Conference: "Rights of New Technologies in the Face of Human Rights Protection", as well as a speaker

Fifth International E-conference: "Man in the face of contemporary threats" presenting the topic: "Breach of personal rights on social networks".

Searching for the answer, references were made to the sources of Polish law, case law, studies and comments on the issue under discussion, as well as articles by the author of the study regarding threats resulting from the use of modern information technologies, which form the basis for further considerations.

The topic of the work was not chosen accidentally. In today's world, where every day demands a guarantee of respect for dignity, and on the other, the image of other people is unlawfully used, it seems that both the current users of social networking sites, as well as the deceased, should investigate this topic. Unauthorized exploitation of third-party goods is a problem that becomes - as Polish case-law indicates - is current and will continue to evolve along with the development of information technology and the emergence of further social networking sites where personal rights violations, such as image, occur.

The method applied at work corresponds to its substantive layout, closing in three chapters. Each of them refers to the issue of the discussed proceedings. It also pointed to the problems that arise in the case of solutions adopted in the field of image protection on social networks.

According to the formulated work objective, appropriate research methods were used: source criticism and analytical and synthetic method.

In the first of these, the author indicates an attempt to define the image. Thanks to this treatment, convergent elements of several definitions are indicated. Attention was focused on a diversified approach to the issue under discussion. The methods of protection of personal rights against the background of the provisions of the Civil Code, the Act on Copyright and Related Rights, or the Act on the Protection of Personal Data and the EU Directive dealing with these issues are indicated.

In the second chapter, the author undertakes to characterize the violations of the image on social networks of natural persons. Indicated, among others the subject of protection, related rights, as well as restrictions on the right to the image. The next section discusses the issue of protective claims in the event of a violation of the right to the image.

The subject of considerations in the third chapter is the protection of personal good - image - post mortem. The author draws attention to the deceased person in Polish law as well as the problem of post mortem image protection. The legal aspects of post-mortem image protection, especially "dead accounts" on social networks were analyzed, as well as the concept of protection of the deceased's personal rights different from the concept of personal good and remembrance of the deceased.

The author summarized the entire work in the conclusions contained in the conclusion.

The analysis carried out in this work indicates the possibilities of protecting the image of in vivo and post mortem users of social networking sites, as well as its legal value and reception in order to protect other personal goods.

LIST OF SHORTCUTS

Art. - article

Dz. U. - Journal of Laws

kc - civil code

kk - penal code

kp - labor law code

kpc - Code of Civil Procedure

kpk - the Code of Criminal Procedure

KPP - Private Law Quarterly

kro - family and care code

ksh - Code of Commercial Companies

p. - page

LIST OF SHORTCUTS

ROZDZIAŁ I

IMMEDIATE AS A SUBJECT OF PROTECTION

1.1. The concept of image

The concept of image as the good of a person whose protection is guaranteed by the regulations of the Polish state is a preliminary issue. At the beginning it should be stated that there is no normative definition of the image. Of course, the doctrine tries to formulate it. Already S. Ritterman, based on art. 19 of the Act of 29 March 1926 on copyright, he stressed that the concept of image includes the image of a person, and therefore the head, as well as the entire character who personalizes this figure as a natural person. From this proposal - idem per idem - two principles can be drawn: the image is attributed to only one physical person (the subjective scope does not include legal persons), the image can be assigned features that directly personalize a given person as a "carrier".

Creating many definitions of the image did not lead to the development of one and - most importantly - universally binding. However, attention should be paid to the suggestions indicated. E. Wojnicka emphasizes that "the image is visible, physical features of a human being, creating its appearance and allowing the identification of a person among people." According to J. Barta and R. Markiewicz, the term "image" should be understood as an intangible product that using plastic means he presents a recognizable image of the other person (or given persons). The question then arises whether the protection of the image will apply only to the "natural human features", or also those that are artificially added, such as makeup, clothing or a prop. J. Bart and T. Markiewicz indicate that the reception is important and the ability to identify, as they emphasize, a person may distinguish the shape, the color of the eyes, but also wearing glasses, a hairstyle, clothing, props - if, and most importantly in this definition: "in isolation or in connection with other features - are they are characteristic for this person.

" These authors also add that, as a rule, the image of a person is referred to as the image of a person, or a likeness, and the image of a person may sometimes consist of a way of walking, gesturing. They give an example of Charlie Chaplin here[1].

Another attempt to define the image is given by J. Sieńczyło-Chlabicz, who emphasizes that the image is all elements that identify a given individual as a specific physical person, e.g. a tattoo that is characteristic for her, a way of speaking etc. And as emphasized earlier, yes and J. Sieńczyło - Chlabicz mentions that "recognizability of a person is a basic condition for granting protection in a given area, as well as the basic criterion for examining whether the image has been violated. The most important is the impression given to the recipient by a given photograph, namely showing that the viewer sees the image of a particular person"[2]. The author clearly indicates that the image includes not only the physical (visual) image of the person, but also - interestingly - the voice (voiced image) and all the elements that are characteristic of a particular physical person, i.e. the way of speaking and moving. Thus, the author points out the features that distinguish a given person and are perceived in public perception as characteristic, hence they allow identification[3].

K. Stefaniuk stated that since the image is explicitly mentioned as a good in art. 23 k.c., it certainly was the name of the Legislator's will. As it points out, it is impossible to define precisely the concepts to determine intangible assets such as the image, for example. You can only indicate certain features. The author includes them: face and its features and the whole form, which allow to identify a person as a specific physical person. More specifically, he adds that this characteristic must be a characteristic, characteristic only for a person, or a physical image. Such a person combines feelings that make up her psychological life, to which she is protected by, among others, image protection the legislator is going to[4].

Probably the most complete definition of the image is given by T. Grzeszczak, for whom the image is a specific determination of the physical image of a human being, capable of reproduction and sharing [5]. A. Matlak also points to these features, but he adds the requirement to "concretize" the image. He emphasizes that "the image is the" fixing "of the physical image of a human

[1] J. Balcarczyk, dz. cyt., Lex nr 94267.
[2] Tamże.
[3] J. Sieńczyło- Chlabicz, *Przedmiot, podmiot i charakter prawa do wizerunku*, PUG 2003, Nr 8, s. 12.
[4] K. Stefaniuk, *Naruszenie prawa do wizerunku przez rozpowszechnianie podobizny*, PiP 1970 nr 1, s. 64.
[5] Tamże.

being at a given moment by other people besides himself"[6]. It can be safely said that all definitions share the same designation of the concept of the image, and therefore not a living person, but a picture of it that is perceived by other people by fixing it on a medium (mostly photography)[7].

Polish courts have also repeatedly attempted to define the image. In 2005, the Supreme Court stressed that "the image, beyond the physical features visible to the environment, creating the appearance of a given unit and allowing - as it is determined - for its identification among other people, may include additional fixed elements related to the profession, as well as characterization , clothing, way of moving around and contacting the surroundings "[8]. The judgment further indicates that such a definition of image is similar to the term "persona", which in turn gives the opportunity to protect the specific interest of a person who would oppose the dissemination of it, or even associations associated with it, for advertising purposes, not even the likeness but the way you speak, your voice, your name.

In 2009, the Supreme Court stated that "although there is no uniform understanding of the notion of image in the doctrine, the prevailing position is the one in which the perceptible, physical features of a human being that make up their appearance and identify a person among people prevail, as physical image, portrait, recognizable image "[9].

Summing up the considerations on the concept of the image itself, it should be recognized that it covers all elements that identify a given individual as a concrete natural person that allows the person to be recognized by others. An image should be understood as a certain mapping of a person's physicality together with its characteristic features that enable identification in a society. Therefore, it is necessary to repeat that the decisive criterion of the notion of image is recognizability.

1.2. Image and the subject of protection of personal rights

[6] E. Ferenc - Szydełko, w: E. Ferenc - Szydełko (red.), *Ustawa o prawie autorskim i prawach pokrewnych. Komentarz, art. 81*, Warszawa 2015, s. 554.
[7] Tamże.
[8] Wyrok SN z 20.05.2005 r., sygn. II CK 330/03, Biuletyn SN 2004 nr 11, s. 10.
[9] Wyrok SN z 15.10.2009 r., sygn. I CSK 72/09, OSNC 2010 nr 1, poz. 29.

The personal property is subject to protection in various branches of law.[10]. And although the concept of personal good has not been defined in the Constitution or in the Civil Code, it should be noted that art. 23 k.c. it provides an example of their enumeration and protection. The personal goods of man are according to the code of k.c. in particular: health, freedom, honor, freedom of conscience, surname or pseudonym, secret of correspondence, inviolability of a flat, scientific, artistic, inventive, rationalizing work. The subject of personal rights is very wide and wide[11].

There seems to be a fundamental formulation of the concept of "good." Literature indicates that "good" is to serve people in order to meet their life needs, but - what is important - in a normative sense, and therefore which there are legal regulations.[12]

In order to define a personal good, it should be emphasized at the outset that initially, when defining the essence of personal rights, the subjective criterion was indicated as dominant, and so the emphasis was placed on the feelings of the person demanding legal protection.[13]. S. Grzybowski also pointed out that personal goods are individual values of a person, his feelings or mental state [14]. Nowadays the view is indicated that when analyzing the essence of personal rights or their violation, one should use an objective criterion, referring to the assessments that were adopted in society[15]. Personal goods understood in this way include the legal system of values, embracing the mental and physical integrity of a person, his individuality, dignity, or social position, which are the premises of his self-fulfillment.[16].

The case law also finds attempts to determine the definition of personal rights. In 1968, the Supreme Court specified personal rights as values related to the inner side of human life, which can not be measured equally, but which are subject to civil protection in the event of their unlawful infringement or threat[17]. In turn, in 1984, it was pointed out that "an open catalog of personal rights also includes

---

[10] J. Kremis, w: *Podstawy prawa cywilnego*, E. Gniewek (red.), Warszawa 2011, s. 48.
[11] S. Grzybowski, *Ochrona dóbr osobistych według przepisów ogólnych prawa cywilnego*, Warszawa 1957, s. 78.
[12] S. Sołtysiński, *Charakter prawny wynalazcy*, Poznań 1967, s. 119.
[13] K. Grzybczyk, *Naruszenie dobra osobistego w reklamie*, „Rejent" 1999, nr 9, s. 120.
[14] S. Grzybowski, dz. cyt., s. 78.
[15] M. Pazdan, w : *Kodeks cywilny. Komentarz do artykułów 1-449*, K. Pietrzykowski (red.), Warszawa 2016, s. 119.
[16] Z. Radwański, *Prawo cywilne- część ogólna,* Warszawa 1997, s. 148.
[17] Wyrok SN z dnia 19 września 1968 r., II CR 291/68.

personal goods related to the sphere of private and family life, with the sphere of intimacy".[18]

Personal goods are, in a way, a distinctive feature of every physical person, they are inseparable and inseparable from it [19].

When discussing personal rights, their basic features should not be overlooked. First of all, it should be stated that these goods are of non-property character, which means that they are subject to intangible goods, which means that they can not be disclosed in the economic category. It should be emphasized that this non-property nature does not change even when their infringement brings financial consequences. Another feature of personal rights is the fact that they are strictly related to the subject that is protected. This means that they arise and go out with it. You can not get rid of them, because you can not separate them from a particular person. Personal goods are also non-hereditary. However, which is quite broadly described in chapter III of the study, some of the rights of a deceased person may be performed by close persons. Then they are treated as subjective rights of the deceased's family. Civil law indicates that personal rights, which are absolute rights, serve the protection of personal rights. Hence, another trait of personal rights is the result, namely the ruthless nature of rights arising from them, an effective erga omnes[20].

In summary, according to art. 23 k.c.[21], the image is the personal good of man. There are various definitions of personal interests in Polish doctrine and science. However, they share a common feature of assigning them a category of values. The subject of the study is not to discuss individual personal rights, however, the introduction is necessary in order to better understand the concept of image as a personal good of every person and to discuss the forms of its protection on social networks.

1.3. Legal protection of the image

[18] Wyrok SN z dnia 18 stycznia 1984 r., I CR 400/83, OSN 1984, poz. 195.
[19] Z. Radwański, dz. cyt., s. 122.
[20] S. Dmowski, S. Rudnicki, *Komentarz do Kodeksu cywilnego. Księga pierwsza. Część* ogólna, Warszawa 2015, s. 110.
[21] Ustawa z dnia 23 kwietnia 1964 r. - Kodeks cywilny (tj. Dz.U. 2016 poz. 380).

The regime of image protection has been expressed in art. 81 of the Act of 4 February 1994 on copyright and related rights [22] (hereinafter: p.a.). It is a general prohibition on spreading someone's image without the consent of the person depicted on it, except: - a well-known person whose image has been made in connection with the performance of public functions, in particular political, social and professional functions; - a person who is only a detail of the whole, such as assembly, landscape, and public event. However, it should be emphasized that the dissemination of the image without prior consent is allowed under the lex specialis, e.g. arrest warrants, defendants in the courtroom. Another issue is in the absence of a clear reservation also the permit is not required when the person depicted on the image received a remuneration, and thus payment for posing [23].

t is indicated above, there is no uniform definition of the image. It was also indicated that it is possible to obtain its protection on the basis of various legal acts. Therefore, the question is whether the image should be treated in the same way on the basis of civil law and copyright law. A. Matlak indicates that in such a case systematic and teleological interpretation should be used and a uniform understanding of the concept of image should be adopted on the basis of both legal acts. Therefore, the task of art. 81 p.a. the task is to specify the regime of this protection provided for in the provisions of the Civil Code. A different understanding of the notion of image would only bring about many difficulties with regard to interpretation[24].

Another view is presented by E. Traple who, referring to T. Grzeszak, indicates that the notion of image is indicated in art. 23 k.c. is wider and defines the image of a human figure, also character traits, behaviors that arise in society, in turn, copyright law should only distinguish the mapping of human characteristics, or - as it adds - props that allow the recognition of a person. Thus, in the case of an image, a cumulative overlap of legal provisions occurs. Civil law norms protect the image of a man in public perception, privacy, and copyright law decides on the recognition of exclusivity in disposing of a person's image and protection of the property interest with this[25].

---

[22] Tj. Dz. U. 2017 poz. 880.

[23] Z. Radwański, A. Olejniczak, *Prawo cywilne - część ogólna*, Warszawa 2011, s. 163.; M. Majos, *Ochrona wizerunku i danych osobowych na portalach społecznościowych*, s. 159.

[24] A. Matlak, *Cywilnoprawna ochrona wizerunku*, KPP 2004, z. 2, s. 321-322.

[25] E. Traple, *Dobra osobiste w reklamie...*, s. 813.

Most of the doctrine shares the opinion of E. Trapie and indicates that the provisions of the Civil Code protect the personal interests of man, and copyright property rights. It should be agreed that the understanding of the notion of image should be harmonized and supportive for broad understanding. It would be worth - as other commentators also point out - to accept the postulate of transferring the provisions on the image from the Copyright Act to the Civil Code. A similar position is taken by, for example, J. Bart and R. Markiewicz, Civil Law Codification Commission in the Green Book of the Civil Code[26], or J. Sieńczyło-Chlabicz.

The doctrine indicates that the provisions on the image in copyright are regulated for historical reasons and do not have any rational justification. The vast majority of commentators investigated by the author mention that especially the norms regarding the image and correspondence should not only be applied to the work, but also to a letter or message sent through a social network which, for example, is not a work[27]. It seems that transferring the provisions from copyright to the Civil Code would give greater coherence and transparency [28].

1.4. *Image protection and personal data*

The source of personal data protection has its source in the Constitution of the Republic of Poland of April 2, 1997.[29] Article 47 clearly states that everyone has the right to protection of private life, family life, honor and good name and the right to decide about his personal life. However, art. 51 directly guarantees data protection for every Polish citizen:

1. No one may be obliged to disclose information relating to him personally other than pursuant to the Act.
2. Public authorities may not obtain, collect and make available other information on citizens than are necessary in a democratic state ruled by law.

---

[26] *Zielona Księga. Optymalna wizja Kodeksu cywilnego w Rzeczpospolitej Polskiej*, Z. Radwański (red.), Warszawa 2006, s. 40.

[27] Podobnie: J. Barta, R. Markiewicz, czy K. Stefaniuk, inaczej wskazuje E. Wojnicka.

[28] J. Sieńczyło- Chlabicz, *Prawo do wizerunku...*, dz. cyt., s. 19.

[29] Dz.U. Nr 78, poz. 483, sprost. Dz.U. Nr 117, poz. 557 ze zmianami.

3. Everyone has the right of access to official documents and data files concerning him. The limitation of this right may be specified by statute.
4. Everyone has the right to demand the rectification and removal of untrue, incomplete or collected information in a manner inconsistent with the Act.

According to art. 6 § 1 of the Act of 29 August 1997 on the protection of personal data[30] "personal information shall be deemed to mean all information relating to an identified or identifiable natural person".

As the standards clearly indicate, an identifiable person is a person whose identity can be identified directly or indirectly, in particular by reference to an identification number or one or more specific factors defining its physical, physiological, mental, economic, cultural or social characteristics. The information is not considered to enable the identification of a person if it would require excessive costs, time or actions. "

The concept of personal data therefore contains three premises. First of all information, and thus all messages: messages, presentations or statements, expressed or recorded in any way (ie, graphic signs, symbols, etc.). Second: it must apply to a natural person. The last premise is the identification or the possibility of identification. G. Shpor advocates a broad definition of information, describing it as a transferable good (non-material), which reduces uncertainty[31].

One can not disagree with J. Barta, P. Fajgielski and R. Markiewicz that personal data are all information that relates to an identified person or which can be identified, and therefore not only information that identifies itself. It should be noted that certainly one information as such will not allow for the identification of a given person, excluding photo or genetic code[32]. The indicated authors also recognize that "all information" serves to emphasize the fact that they refer to every aspect of a person, personal or material relations, professional, private, scientific or eg character traits[33].

It should be emphasized that personal data can not be considered - within the meaning of the Act - messages about a person (character) unrealistic, fictional, fairy tale, from a novel, movie or games, etc.[34]

---

[30] Ustawa z dnia 29 sierpnia 1997 r. o ochronie danych osobowych (tj. Dz.U. 2016 poz. 922).
[31] G. Szpor, *Pojęcie informacji a zakres danych osobowych*, w: P. Fajgielski (red.), *Ochrona danych osobowych w Polsce z perspektywy dziesięciolecia*, Lublin 2008, s. 8.
[32] J. Barta, P. Fajgielski, R. Markiewicz, *art. 6,* w: J. Barta, P. Fajgielski, R. Markiewicz, *Ochrona danych osobowych. Komentarz*, Warszawa 2011, Lex nr 106637.
[33] Tamże.
[34] M. Majos, dz. cyt., s. 164.

It has been pointed out above that the second premise on personal data information must relate to a natural person [35], whose identity is fixed or determinable. The above mentioned authors put it this way: "it is important that, apart from the field of interest, he places information collections (included eg in the form of registers and records) concerning entities other than physical persons, and thus all organizational units, regardless of whether they have they have legal personality (including clubs, associations, informal groups), state and local government administration bodies and others. This is not an accepted assumption, but it exists in many foreign laws on the protection of personal data (eg in the German and French laws), as well as in Directive 95/46 / EC[36].

The decision of the Supreme Administrative Court of 18 November 2009 is important because of the protection of the image on social networks, in which the court clearly indicates that the image of a person marked in a class photograph made thirty years ago with the name and surname, and then placed on the website constitutes personal data within the meaning of art. 6 par. 2 of the Act on the Protection of Personal Data. The assessment of whether the identification of an identity requires excessive costs, time or actions should be made taking into account technical capabilities while processing personal data.[37]. Earlier, in this judgment, personal data were indicated: "a team of messages (messages) about a specific person so integrated that it allows him to be personalized. It includes at least the information necessary to identify (name, surname, place of residence), however this is not limited as it also contains further information, enhancing the level of identification"[38].

Thus, the inclusion of a class photo from 30 years ago on the social networking site raises the issue of the admissibility of sharing photos with images of other people. The NSA indicated that such a photograph is protected by personal data, which also applies to drawings or films. It should be pointed out that the portal administrator should supervise the proper protection of personal data. It is on him that he is obliged to pay due attention to appropriate privacy settings, and then deleting data from inactive users or after closing their account[39].

---

[35] Dane osobowe osoby prawnej chronione są w kodeksie cywilnym o ochronie dóbr osobistych osób prawnych (art. 43 k.c.) oraz niektórych ustaw szczegółowych.
[36] J. Barta, P. Fajgielski, R. Markiewicz, dz. cyt., Lex nr 106637.
[37] Wyrok NSA w Warszawie z 19.05.2011 r., sygn. I OSK 1079/10, Lex nr 990136.
[38] Tamże.
[39] M. Majos, dz. cyt., s. 167.

CHAPTER II

PROTECTION OF IMAGE OF USERS OF COMMUNITY PORTALS

2.1. The right of users of portals to the image

It is extremely difficult to determine the functions and range that the Internet meets today. Dynamic and often unpredictable direction of development with mass exchange of content, photos and materials increase proportionally the risk of violating the rights of third parties. At the very beginning it is worth pointing out which social networking sites are the most popular and try to characterize the right to the image of the portal user, because it will help to identify the areas and groups of people who are most threatened with image violations. Where can we find the most active users? Research indicates that Facebook, Instragram, Tweeter, Nasza Klasa are used most often (currently: nk.pl)[40].

The right to image in literature and jurisprudence is understood in three ways:

1) the law protecting ideal interests, and therefore exposed to violation due to recording, dissemination or distortion of the image in various contexts[41]

2) as an entitlement that creates a monopoly allowing the dissemination of an image resembling rights on intangible goods, then it is about personal rights [42]

3)

as a monistic and therefore mixed - personal and property law, which therefore protects

[40] G. Marciniak, *Cyberprzemoc: zagrożenia związane z użyciem nowoczesnych technologii informacyjnych*, w: V. Tanaś, W. Welskop (red.), *Edukacja w zglobalizowanym świecie*, Łódź 2016, s. 332.

[41] A. Lucas-Schlotter, w: A. Ohly, H. Beverly-Smith, A. Lucas - Schlotter, *Privacy, Property and Personality - Civil Law Pespectives on Commercial Appropriation*, Cambridge 2005, s. 156-159.

[42] J. Berta, *Prawo do wizerunku i prawo adresata do korespondencji*, w: SPP tom 13, Warszawa 2017, s. 775.

personal interests and creates a monopoly of exploitation, which is not transferable, and the subject of the license are property rights [43].

In Poland, protection of the interests of the user of a social networking site regarding the image in the civil law market - as has already been pointed out - is regulated in many legal acts. However, the Civil Code indicated is of fundamental importance. This protection does not exclude civil law protection provided for in other regulations, in accordance with art. 24 § 3 k.c .. First and foremost, these are:

1) art. 81-83 p.a.

2) art. 13 para. 2 and 3, art. 14 para. 1, 3, 5-6, article 31 a- 33 of the press law,

3) art. 14 of the Act on the provision of electronic services

In addition, detailed provisions can be found in substantive criminal law - art. 191 a, 202§4b, art. 212-216 and 267 KK, lawsuit - art. 279-280 CCP and administrative (eg Articles 23-35 of the Act on the Protection of Personal Data).

The indicated provisions restrict this right due to public interest, or strengthen it in specific cases with criminal sanctions.

The right to decide on the possibility of distributing the image of users of social networking sites is to a large extent protected under the right to privacy on the basis of art. 23-24 k.c., for whom the limitation is freedom of speech and the right to information. The protection of these goods is indicated in the Constitution in art. 47 and 54. Conventions that protect human rights also provide for the protection of goods:

1) European Convention for the Protection of Human Rights and Fundamental Freedoms of 4 November 1950.

2) The International Covenant on Civil and Political Rights of December 16, 1966.

2.2. Permissions of social network users

From the point of view of social networks, the most susceptible to violations are image, company or name, surname, sphere of privacy. Violation of the image on social networking sites usually consists in harming its image by disseminating the image without its consent, ridicule and humiliation through the "correction" of the image.

---

[43] Tamże.

It has already been noted that the subject of protection is the image, the concept of which is discussed in chapter I. The relationship between the image and the object of protection of personal rights is also indicated. In these paragraphs, the author will focus on the rights of users of social networking sites.

First of all, the right to prohibit the fixation or distortion of the image should be indicated. These actions constitute a violation of personal rights only when it compromises the privacy of the subject or the cult of the memory of a loved one, clearly protected by the code of ...

The protection of the rightholder will be granted only if it is not demonstrated that the person acting on the site of the social networking website is unlawful. It is worth adding here that a satirical depiction of an image may be allowed if it concerns the freedom of artistic expression[44].

Another right is the right to decide on the dissemination of the image. Prohibition of the dissemination of the image may be formulated on the basis of both art. 23 k.c., as well as art. 81 p.a .. However, it should be noted whether the scope of both provisions is the same. It is assumed that from art. 23 k.c. it should be concluded that not every distribution of the user's image will violate the personal law. Protection will be granted only if the unlawfulness of violation of personal interest is demonstrated, which is connected with the idea of protecting man as such. It should be remembered that property interests are protected in a derivative manner, i.e. in addition to personal interests and only on the basis of tort liability. Returning, however, to the personal interest described, it should be noted that the personal interest may be violated due to honor, privacy, etc. As rightly noted by Barta, the question arises about the desirability of a separate personal right to the image. However, as he points out, deciding on the dissemination of an image always has an ideal value, and sometimes also an asset value[45].

Pointing further to the literal and systemic interpretation of art. 81 p.a. it is necessary to formulate the right of the user of the social networking site more radical than indicated in the Civil Code. Pursuant to this provision, any (except as provided in the Act) dissemination of an image without consent or permission is a violation of personal or property interest. Such protection can only be refused in principle only on the basis of art. 5th c.: "You can not make use of your right that would be contrary to

[44] Zob. Wyrok SN z 5 listopada 2008 r., sygn. akt I CSK 164/08, Legalis.
[45] Szerzej: J. Barta, *Prawo do wizerunku...*, dz. cyt., s. 797.

the socio-economic destiny of this law or the principles of social coexistence. Such act or omission of the rightholder is not regarded as exercising the right and does not benefit from protection. '

It is clear from the doctrine that the dissemination of the image is treated as violation of the right to the image[46]. However, none of the authors indicated does not form the view that the right of the user of the social networking site creates a legal monopoly of exploitation on his part. J. Błeszyński notes that "publishing a photograph or someone else's portrait," one enters into another sphere of personal rights, the right to likeness "[47]. There is no indication, however, whether subsequent publications, expanding the field of exploitation is a violation of this right. It should be noted that only one author indicated the concept of the right to image in art. 81 p.a. as permission to use the image [48]. The second commentator criticizes such an assumption as the intangible assets that do not take into account the numerus clausus principle. It should be emphasized that the problem is not to create ex nihilo rights on an intangible good, but on the interpretation of statutory solutions, allowing to see the potential. It should be noted that the legislator himself created an absolute right to the image[49].

The right of the user of the social networking site to decide on the dissemination of the image allows to protect both the personal and property interest. An analogy to copyright law needs to be emphasized, where it not only protects against violation of personal interest, but also grants the user power over an external, immaterial thing that is associated with him. The portals user may distribute the image himself or may allow other participants of the virtual world to do so. It should be emphasized that he can not just get rid of this right definitively[50].

From art. 81 p.a. You can distinguish other possible approaches to the right to the image, namely:

1) as a rule that removes the collision of copyright with the personal rights of a user of a social networking site;

2) the right to decide on making the image publicly available.

---

[46] Tu należy wskazać np.: F. Zoll, *Polska ustawa o prawie autorskim*, s. 71; K. Grzybczyk, *Naruszanie...*, dz. cyt., s. 128 czy J. Balcarczyk, dz. cyt., s. 131.

[47] J. Błeszyński, *Prawo autorskie,* Warszawa 1988, s. 154.

[48] Zob. J. Barta, R. Markiewicz, *Wokół prawa...*, dz. cyt., s. 19.

[49] J. Barta, *Prawo do wizerunku...*, dz. cyt., s. 798.

[50] Tamże.

Investigating the idea of the first intake of art. 81 p.a. it should be pointed out that in order to disseminate the image one should obtain the permission of a portrayed subject. If the norm of art. 81 p.a. it would be treated only as a collision-removing rule, then a portrayed person would only be allowed to disseminate his image that would violate any personal law in connection with art. 23 and 24 k.c ..

It is generally accepted that the right to image contained in art. 81 p.a. is the concretisation of the law from art. 23 k.c .. However, it should be emphasized that it is the protection of the ideal interest that the user of the social networking site has to decide on the dissemination of the image. And here the indication requires that it is independent of whether it involves a violation of other goods[51].

Art. 81 p.a. clearly indicates the permission to disseminate the image. The grammatical interpretation of this provision makes it possible to say that this is a 'as such' license, not everyone, as indicated by J. Bart, a specific territorial time stage, etc. The user's right of Article 81 would protect the personal interest he has in the right to decide whether and which image is to be made public It is worth to point out the voice of T. Grzeszak[52] o the judgment of August 28, 1996. In the judgment of April 11, 2001[53] the court granted protection to the privacy of the infringer in connection with the unauthorized disclosure of the files found in the apartment. According to the court, the image was not disseminated on the basis of art. 81 p.a., because the pictures were in the possession of one person.

It should be pointed out that the image is "owned" by the person portrayed, and therefore is the subject of his authority, protected against unauthorized persons, regardless of whether or not the violation of the ideal interest discussed above is demonstrated.[54].

2.3. Recognition and image distribution and authorization

[51] Np. A. Matlak, dz. cyt., s. 321.
[52] T. Grzeszak, glosa do wyroku SA w Łodzi, I ACr 341/96, MoP 1997, Nr 8, s. 318.
[53] Zob. Wyrok SA z dnia 11 kwietnia 2001 r., sygn. akt I ACa 244.01, TPP 2002, Nr 3.
[54] J.Barta, *Prawo do wizerunku...,.,* s. 805.

Before the author moves on to the notion of dissemination and strictly related authorization, he should be pointed to the recognition feature.

The functions of image identification and information require the authorized person to prove that the image has been disseminated and is recognizable on it. In the doctrine, there is no uniform view as to the level of recognition, namely whether it is enough for the image to recognize the authorized entity and people from its environment, or whether it must also be recognized by other persons. Therefore, two aspects of recognizability should be distinguished: the way of presenting a physical person, that is, a set of features that enable its identification as well as recipients of such a performance[55].

The first aspect - for J. Sieńczyło-Chlabicz - is the way of receiving the image, whether the recipient is aware of the fact that he sees a specific person. The author indicates that the norms of copyright do not define the level of recognition, nor do they provide features that are to facilitate identification. Therefore, the most important role in recognition is played by the face, but no less important are other features that facilitate the identification of the person, e.g. as already mentioned before - the way of moving around[56].

Regarding the second aspect - and therefore the group of people for whom the image must be recognizable in order to be able to provide legal protection, J. Sieńczyło-Chlabicz advocates hypothetical recognition as minimal, but also sufficient to provide such protection. It indicates here the analysis of German solutions. And he adds that a sufficient premise of protection is recognition by the circle of close relatives[57].

Mr. Grzeszak emphasizes a bit differently, pointing out that granting legal protection to an image should be made conditional upon the need for similarity, which can be noticed not only by the authorized entity, but also by a third party. The Supreme Court in its judgment of February 27, 2003, points out that recognition must be universal and can not be reduced to the circle of loved ones[58]. T. Grzeszak indicates that in the case of investigation of the protection infringed by the dissemination of the image, it is sufficient for the person to be identified by anyone[59].

---

[55] IV CKN 1819/00, OSP 2004, Nr 6, poz. 75, s. 320.
[56] J. Sieńczyło- Chlabicz, dz. cyt., s. 20.
[57] Tamże.
[58] Wyrok SN z 27 lutego 2003 r., IV ACa 348/03, niepubl.
[59] T. Grzeszak, dz. cyt., s. 542.

J. Barta and R. Markiewicz emphasize that recognizability does not have to be the same as giving data that identifies a natural person (name and surname). In their opinion, it is enough to associate a given person with a specific natural person[60].

Summing up the above views, one should assume that, in the case of an image on social networks, for protection purposes, the requirement of recognition refers to the identification of the closest persons, and the degree of protection should be directly proportional to the level of violation. In the event that personal and property interests are violated, priority should be given to the protection of a natural person.

On the other hand, one should consider whether a better solution would be to consider a solution if the personal interests of the individual were infringed, the identity of the person would be a sufficient identifier of the person, and in the case of a non-material breach could also include third parties.

The case law of the Supreme Court stressed that the violation of the right to the image occurs when the photograph on which a given person is without consent allows him to identify[61].
In order to better illustrate this violation, we should refer to the case from 2003, when the social portal Nasza-Klasa illegally used the images of users. One of them filed a lawsuit, stating that the portal illegally uses his image in the advertising of one of the banks. It should be emphasized here that the issue of personalized ads with names, surnames or pseudonyms is a common practice of social networking sites. When the plaintiff - Krzysztof R. logged into his account, saw his image in a personalized bank credit card ad for him. This visualization was only available to that user, so it was not infringed on Art. 81 par. 1 zd. 1 p.a .. The District Court in Wrocław ruled against the portal, indicating that the image is a personal good, and Krzysztof R., consented to the registration of the profile, to use the image for social purposes, and not for marketing purposes. The amount of PLN 5,000 was then awarded, which was much lower than demanded by the plaintiff. It should be pointed out that such a low amount in the verdict could be much higher, then it may deter other portals from similar practice. Dissemination of the image means making it available through any medium. In connection with the framework of the study, the author will focus on sharing on social networks. It should be pointed out that the requirement of public access is important, and is therefore intended for a wider, undefined group of people. It should be

[60] J. Barta, R. Markiewicz, *Wokół prawa do wizerunku...*, s. 13.
[61] Wyrok SN z 27 lutego 2003 r., syg. akt IV CKN 1819/00.

emphasized that such a requirement does not meet the availability of friends in family circles. Although it must be recognized that in certain circumstances, e.g. within one institution, it may violate personal rights[62]. In one of the judgments, it was stated that the short presence of the recording at issue on the Internet did not exclude the possibility of other people getting to know it.

It is also worth pointing out to the generally present storage on your profile on a social portal that someone unlawfully makes someone else's image or the so-called. hypelinku to such an image that does not release from liability, even if the user does not distribute it. It may be liable for damages if it does not block access to other users, at the request of the rightholder[63].

Now, the author will go over to discuss the permission to disseminate the image and its legal character. Granting such permission is the basis for the implementation of the right to the image. Permission to distribute the image is an authorization. It should be pointed out that it must comply with the law and principles of social coexistence, as indicated in art. 58 k.c .. It should be mentioned that the case-law emphasizes that interpretation on such principles is made in the same way as the interpretation of declarations of will. Therefore, when the statement has defects, then the standards with the defects of declarations of will apply[64].

Users of social networking sites should be aware of their consent to the dissemination of the image, as the permission in question does not cover such dissemination, which would not be covered by the awareness of the consequences of a given dissemination for the user's personal rights. This applies in particular to a situation where it is a general permission to disseminate the image in any way, which is evidenced by the case law: "by signing the consent for the publication of photos, it did not include the awareness of the possibility of using these photos for the advertising of audio-text services"[65], as well as when the user of the social networking site has explicitly agreed to use the image in any context: "The permission to use the image must be expressed with awareness of the consequences resulting from it and should refer to specific facts, and thus the specific ways and circumstances of using the image (. ...) the permit can not, therefore, be of an abstract nature"[66]. What is more, the courts

---

[62] Wyrok SA z 24.02.2016 r. sygn akt. I ACa 1630.15, Legalis.
[63] Zob. Orzeczenie Wielkiej Izby ETPCz z 16.06.2015 r., w sprawie Delfi AS v. Estonia 64596/09.
[64] Wyrok SA w Warszawie z 27 października 2005 r., sygn. akt VI ACa 838/04, Legalis.
[65] Zob. wyrok SA z 20 czerwca 2002 r., sygn. akt I ACa 1358.01.
[66] Wyrok SA w Warszawie z 7 maja 2014 r. , sygn. akt I ACa 1686.13, Legalis.

point to the invalidity of the license to the extent that the user was not aware of the consequences, and the dissemination caused a violation of the image or reverence.

It is worth pointing to the postulates of the doctrine here, so that the permissions of network users are not blank consents. However, it should be recognized that the mere dissemination of photographs is then deprived of illegality, due to the purpose or context of dissemination[67].

Another issue concerning the discussed subject is the revocability of consent. It is generally accepted that the authorization is revocable at any time. In the 2007 judgment, the court pointed out that the revocation of consent for the dissemination or disclosure of the image was ex nunc[68].

2.4. Limitations of the right to the image

The rights of users of social networking sites to disseminate their image must sometimes give way to the public's right to information. There are two categories of cases in which the dissemination of the image is allowed without the permission of the person portrayed in accordance with art. 81 par. 2 points 1 and p.a .: 1) when it comes to information about the public activity of well-known people 2) when it is a message of images, the image of gatherings, public events or landscapes, where the image of the individual is only a detail of the whole. When discussing this issue, begin by indicating the scope of "well-known people." A literal interpretation would indicate that such people were first widely known, then freely distribute their images. For this interpretation, among others, K. Stefaniuk, J. Sonczak or J. Sieńczyło-Chlabicz, the Supreme Court pointed out that "the term" circle of people "commonly known >> includes people who directly or implicitly consent to publicizing knowledge about their lives. however, only actors, singers or politicians, but also people conducting other activities, for example economic or social"[69].

[67] Szerzej: J. Barta, *Prawo autorskie...*, s. 810.
[68] Wyrok SA we Wrocławiu z dnia 26 lutego 2007 r., sygn. akt I ACa 1492/06, OSA 2007, Nr 3, poz. 41.
[69] Wyrok SN z 20 lipca 2007 r., sygn. akt I CSK 134.07, Legalis.

The framework of this study concerns the users of social networking sites, so the author deliberately does not indicate the origin of the term "well-known people" or people of common interest, although the second reality is close to users of portals due to the possibility of violations due to the unlawful image of people accompanying in public situations to people who are well-known because of their office or activities they conduct. Special attention - according to the author - requires discussing photos from party events. It is common for entities operating in the field of entertainment services (especially clubs, pubs) to create photo catalogs or videos that show the people at the time of the event, and users of social networks may unlawfully abuse and infringe on someone's image due to the depicted an image of a given natural person. M. Tomczyk even formulates the term "photo-clubbing"[70].

It has been indicated above that persons who are a detail of a larger whole are deprived of the right to decide on the dissemination of their image. The enumeration: assembly, landscape, public event seems to be exhaustive, but it does not deprive the open character of this provision. It is enough to point out that the term "gathering" itself is out of focus, i.e. it can be extended to any larger group of people.The public event is an event that is not closed to a selected group of people. dealing with a perpetuated image of a given person, only that performed during a public event, or staying in the landscape space, the exclusion of this protection does not work.It should be emphasized that there would then be a contradiction with the ratio legis of this norm. "the dissemination of an image does not require a permit if it constitutes only an accidental or accessory element of the whole presented, i.e. if the image is removed, the subject and nature of the performance would not change."[71]

According to the jurisprudence, in the situation of the dissemination of an image that is not singular, but constitutes a sequence stretched over time, the time and purpose of showing a specific physical person will be important.[72]. It is also worth reminding that the ability of the viewer to recognize a given person also becomes a condition. That is why the court in Warsaw treated, for example, a ten-second camera shot on the plaintiff's face, only on the occasion of showing the prison as a violation of his right to image. Similarly, a violation of the right to image was found when in the documentary film the close-up of the face of a particular person was shown

[70] M. Tomczyk, *Foto-clubbing: aspekty prawne*, „Edukacja humanisyczna" nr 1 (26) 2012, Szczecin 2012, s. 171- 179.
[71] Wyrok SA w Krakowie z dnia 19 grudnia 2001 r., sygn. akt I ACa 957/01, TPP 2002, Nr 3, s. 108.
[72] Wyrok SA w Warszawie z dnia 26 listopada 2003 r., sygn. akt VI ACa 384/03, niepubl..

several times[73]. In the judgment of 2010, the violation of the right to the image of a prisoner was found, the face of which was shown for about 2 seconds on television [74]. On the other hand, the two-second shot of the plaintiff - the bus driver - did not violate the advertising rights of the advertising film, according to SA in Warsaw[75].

2.5. *Protective claims in the event of a law violation to the image*

Distinguishing the violation of the image from violation of the right to the image does not make much sense [76]. Indeed, the violation may be related to the personal interest regarding the image, the power over it, and thus the right to the image. As noted earlier, the dissemination of the image may lead to violations of other personal rights. It is worth paying attention to court judgments, where the situation concerns the publication of photos of random people in a false context, or which violates privacy[77].

Regulations of the k.c. they do not infringe the rights indicated in other provisions, namely: art. 78 paragraph 1 p.a. (Article 83 p.a. refers to its appropriate application, Articles 448, 405, 415 k.c.). The coincidence of claims may be an alternative (eg in the situation of redress, apology, compensation for damage to property). It is obvious that if the dissemination of the image by the users of social networks will harm many of the ideal legal interests, this will affect the amount of compensation.

In the case of a threat to the right to protect the image by someone else's action (eg preparing for the publication of a given image), the protection entity may demand discontinuation of action. It can also apply for securing the claim on general terms, and therefore in accordance with art. 730 and n. K.c.

[73] Wyrok SA w Białymstoku z dnia 14 listopada .2012 r., sygn. akt I ACa 543/12, Legalis.
[74] Wyrok SA w Warszawie z dnia 3 grudnia .2010 r., sygn akt VI ACa 725/10, niepubl.
[75] Wyrok SA w Warszawie z dnia 10 lutego 2005 r., sygn. akt I ACa 509/04, niepubl.
[76] J. Barta, *Prawo autorskie.*, s. 834.
[77] Por. wyrok SN z dnia 21 września 1963 r., sygn. akt I CR 734/62, Legalis; wyrok SA w Białymstoku z dnia 6 lutego 1992 r., sygn. akt wyr. SA w Warszawie z 3.4.1997 r., I ACa 148/97, Wok. 1998,Nr 4, s. 40; wyrok SN z dnia 8 stycznia 2004 r., I CK 40/03, Legalis; wyrok SA w Warszawie z dnia 20 czerwca 2002 r., sygn. akt I ACa 1358/01, Wok. 2003, Nr 10; wyrok. SN z dnia 4 lutego 2005 r., sygn. akt I CK 515/04, Legalis; wyr. SA w Warszawie z dnia 19 maja .2005 r., sygn. akt I ACa 788/04, Legalis.

The claim to stop the infringement, and thus to stop sharing, dissemination is, of course, to limit the negative effects of such an infringement. The removal of the consequences may consist in submitting a statement by the infringer in the relevant content, eg explanation, regrets or apologies. It is worth emphasizing here that also the victim himself may act and have a request to publish his answer or rectification[78].

One of the basic problems related to the right to image protection is the regulation of the so-called the economic exploitation of the image and the concept of commercialization. This situation has no regulation either under international law or under national law. Of course, individual actions are taken, which, however, are far from the general regulation of the issue in question[79]. Meanwhile, the situation is developing very dynamically, especially when it comes to social media portals and the fact that new areas of research are being created as a result of the development of new forms of image violations - and therefore the need to regulate this issue. Especially recently, when there are more and more types of commercialization, the protection of the image is not only the image of the person who gives such consent, but also people who are often unaware that their image has been used for a specific action.

It should be mentioned here that using the image in every unlawful form is subject to the regime of K.C. or other acts - depending on the form of the violation and the object of the good that was infringed, as well as the person concerned. In the case of a photo, this may be a violation of both the image of the person shown in the photograph and the copyright infringement of the author of the photograph. There are no specific regulations regarding individual forms of using an illegal image depending on various forms of this use - therefore in some situations, despite the dissemination of a given image on the Internet, such action will not be understood as dissemination causing liability, as not always dissemination in a small group it will violate the image of a given person, as discussed later in this chapter. If you are active in the event of a violation of personal rights, it is usually a person whose personal rights have been violated. In the case of people who do not have full legal capacity (children or persons incapacitated), they will be parents, legal guardians, probation officers. In the event of violation of the right to the image

[78] J. Barta, *Prawo autorskie.*, s. 835.
[79] K. Osajda (red.), *Kodeks cywilny*; również J. Balcarczyk, *Prawo do wizerunku i jego komercjalizacja,* Warszawa 2009.

of the deceased person, persons with an intern's ID will be heirs who then act on their behalf in the protection of the personal good, which is the cult of the deceased. Identifying passive ID - this is determining who should be sued for a lawsuit, can sometimes cause problems. Often people may not know that their image circulates somewhere on dating sites or in other internet spaces and often serves unlawful purposes. The image begins to live its own life. The person may not know about the use of the image or he may learn quite by accident. Only then can he take certain steps.

Always a passive player is always passive[80]. On the terms regulated by separate regulations, they will not be services provided electronically because their liability is excluded by law. The Supreme Court, interpreting art. 14 para. 1 of the Act on the provision of electronic services in the judgment of 8 July 2011[81], He pointed out that the service provider providing services consisting in providing free access to the discussion portal he created is not liable for infringement of third party goods, unless he knew that the entry on the portal infringed these goods and did not remove it immediately. According to the press law, the civil liability for violation of the law caused by the publication of the press material is borne by the author, editor or other person who caused the publication of this material; it does not exclude - of course - the responsibility of the publisher. It should be remembered that in the area of financial liability, the liability of these persons is joint and several. Summing up the considerations regarding the unlawfulness of the violations of the image, it should be emphasized that at present court cases are recognized on the basis of general civil law and copyright law, tort liability provisions and liability for unfair competition acts. A party who asserts its rights may assert them both on the basis of k.c. and p.a., which is important - parallel and independently. One act can be the subject of protection in several areas.

According to art. 24 k.c .: the one whose personal good is threatened by someone else's actions, can:

1) demand the abandonment of this action, unless it is not unlawful;

2) demand that the person who committed the violation should complete the actions necessary to remove its consequences;

[80] M. Brzozowska, *Naruszenie dóbr osobistych w Internecie na forach internetowych*, MoP 2014, Nr 2, s. 1189; por. *Ł. Goździaszek, Prawo blogosfery*, Warszawa 2014.

[81] Wyrok SN z dnia 8 lipca 2011r, sygn. akt IV CSK 665/10, OSNC 2012, Nr 2, poz. 27.

3) demand that the infringer declares the appropriate content and in the appropriate form.

In addition, under the rules provided for in the Code, he may also demand financial compensation or payment of an appropriate sum of money for the indicated social purpose. If a property damage has been caused as a result of a personal property infringement, the aggrieved party may request it to be remedied on general terms.
The above standards do not infringe the rights provided for in other regulations, in particular in the p.a. and in inventive law. The protection of the image in copyright is regulated by art. 83 p.a. It orders for this purpose to apply the provisions of art. 78 paragraph 1 pa. On this basis, the person whose image is harmed is entitled to a claim to cease activities that pose a threat to the image, claim to complete the actions necessary to remove the effects of the violation - in particular, submit a statement of appropriate content and form, and in addition, if the violation occurred and if the breach was a fault, a claim for payment of an appropriate sum of money for compensation for the non-material harm suffered or a corresponding sum of money for the social purpose indicated by the plaintiff.

CHAPTER III

PROTECTION OF POST MORTEM

3.1. The concept of protection of the deceased's personal rights

In Polish doctrine, the conviction that personal rights with death expires. Although this view is dominant, attention should be paid to the possibility of post-mortem personal rights. Most often, this view can be found in the literature in connection with art. 78 paragraph 2 p.a .. However, there is a discrepancy between the authors. It is worth pointing to the judgment of SA in Warsaw - VI Civil Department of 27.10.2011.[82], where it is emphasized that those close to the deceased should apply for the protection of their own personal rights (that is, subjective rights) due to the linking relationship with the deceased. Nevertheless, the sentence of J. Barta and R. Markiewicz seems to be accurate, who clearly indicate that the death of the creator does not allow to state that the personal goods that belonged to the ante mortem person. The indicated authors also emphasize that at the moment of death, there is also no transfer of personal rights of the relatives who died in the personal rights of his relatives[83]. Of course, according to the law of inheritance, the entities, as a rule, entitled to claim protection of these goods, are the spouse - or - descendants, ascendants or siblings and descendants of siblings [84]. It should be noted here that the link of the author after his death with the work is slowly narrowed, but the right to protection of goods, like the right to authorship, is still protected [85].

As noted by Z. Lisowska, the most emphatic view of the non-expiry of personal rights along with the death, emphasizes J. Mazurkiewicz [86]. The author analyzing the issue discussed in the work [87] points out that a distinction should be made between the personal property of the deceased and the personal rights associated with that person,

---

[82] Sygn. VI ACa 461/11. Legalis.
[83] J. Barta, R. Markiewicz, *Prawo autorskie,* Warszawa 2013, s. 107-108.
[84] P. Sobolewski, w: *Kodeks cywilny...,* s. 391.
[85] J. Barta, R. Markiewicz, *Prawo...,* dz. cyt., s. 107-108.
[86] Z. Lisowska, *Dobra osobiste zmarłych i możliwość ich ochrony w Internecie,* PME nr 2/2016, s. 44.
[87] J. Mazurkiewicz, *Non omnis moriar...,* s. 26.

and that[88]. An important argument for the protection of personal rights post mortem seems to be the fact that the constitutional protection of dignity, including its violation, can not cease with the moment of death, and as emphasized by other authors, it seems more significant at the time, including for the sake of the ethical values of society[89]. Embossing requires that protection of non-proprietary values by post mortem should be possible precisely because of the dignity of the human person. As J. Mazurkiewicz points out, the doctrine adopted in the doctrine of protection of personal rights of deceased persons only through the possibility of their protection by relatives in the form of the deceased person's memory and memory, as it also seems to the author, insufficient and completely ineffective, because it protects only selected personal rights or it can also lead to violations of the deceased's will. An example of this is putting religious symbols on the tombstone of a deceased person, despite her obvious previous opposition to such gestures[90].

According to the above, it should be pointed out that the entity that could claim rights in respect of violations of the personal rights of the deceased person could be - as J. Mazurkiewicz points out - a special curator (or even several). The appointment of such a person would take place by the deceased ante mortem or by the court, if that was the will of the deceased. The discussed approach or solution would certainly be a departure from the need to represent the deceased by the representative, because the personal good of the deceased would be the object of protection, not the personal good of the living person. In the absence of the appointment of a guardian by a deceased person to claim protection of personal rights, the heirs may be eligible[91]. The indicated concept did not find only supporters, but also opponents who recognized the appointment of such a curator impossible to introduce and - because of economic reasons - impractical, because it would have to be financed by someone, controlled, if in the event of transgression, someone would have to decide on this violation and react in a way to them[92].

When the claim is made that, with death, not all of the deceased person's personal goods go out, then a catalog of the most important goods that would deserve

---

[88] Tamże, s. 23-24.

[89] Zob. K. Skubisz- Kępka, *Ochrona nazwiska zmarłego jako dobra osobistego*, w: J. Balcarczyk (red.), *Dobra osobiste w XXI wieku*, Warszawa 2012, s. 430.

[90] J. Mazurkiewicz, *Non omnis moriar...*, s. 23.

[91] Tamże, s. 35-36.

[92] M. Wilejczyk, *Zagadnienia etyczne części ogólnej prawa cywilnego*, Warszawa 2014, s. 174-175.

post mortem protection and, of course, can be characterized.[93]. Of course, this is about those goods that are in a different way than the loved ones who are born for the loved ones. Due to the indicated essence of goods, it should be pointed out at the outset that the deceased will not be entitled to personal good, such as protection of life and health, but others - such as the right to name and surname, correspondence protection, copyright, and finally the image - require and certainly they deserve protection[94]. J. Mazurkiewicz mentions the possibility of protecting personal property such as image, personal rights of the employee, protection of correspondence, placing the name in the company of a legal person, company or company of a natural person[95].

The above-mentioned concept, despite the difference from the concept of good protection of the memory and worship of the deceased person, allows to emphasize the fact that such protection would be more complete and certainly more identifiable with the will of the individual after her death.

Other authors emphasize that protection of the deceased's image, clearly indicated in art. 83 p.a., and also limited there, is a compromise[96]. T. Grzeszak emphasizes that just at the moment of death, the legal subjectivity of a person is also lost, so that his personal rights are lost with it. However, after a while he also adds that "therefore the theoretical justification of the right to image understood as a personal good after the death of the rightholder is the subject of discussion in the doctrine." On the other hand, K. Święcicka and JS Święcicki state that despite the loss of the right to the image of the deceased, these rights are also claimed after the death of persons mentioned in Article 78 (2), ie the spouse, in its absence in turn to children, parents, children of siblings "[97]. The restriction referred to above is the prevention of the implementation of unlimited personal rights of the creator of the image, and above all out of concern for the use of its expiration of author's proprietary rights. As J. Berta and R Markiewicz point out: "the more appropriate place for this kind of provisions was the Civil Code"[98]. However, in this study, the author focuses primarily on protecting the image of the deceased.

[93] Z. Lisowska, *Dobra osobiste...*, s. 44.
[94] J. Mazurkiewicz, *Czy dobra osobiste mogą powstać po śmierci?,* w: J. Balcarczyk (red.), dz. cyt., s. 421-422.
[95] Tamże; Z. Lisowska, *Dobra osobiste...*, s. 45.
[96] Szerzej: T. Grzeszak, *Treść prawa do wizerunku i prawa adresata do korespondencji*, w: SPP, s. 514.
[97] .,,Prawa autorskie..., s. 140
[98] J. Barta, R, Markiewicz, w: J. Barta, M. Czajkowska- Dąbrowska, s. 384-385.

3.2. The mechanism of post mortem image protection on social networks

The rapid development of the Internet requires effective protection of personal rights of deceased people. The effect of a person's death is not always limited only to the real world, but also to information (image) in a virtual reality. In the work, the author examines image protection, so the personal good appears to be basic, which can be violated on the Internet. The widespread presence of photos on the Internet, the ease of their modification, or the possibility of sharing them is the basis for reflection on the post-mortem image protection mechanism. It is worth pointing out that the image is also subject to the phenomenon of commercialization, which intensifies this type of infringement of the personal good, especially the deceased person.

Chapter II indicates the users of the virtual world, their activity, who due to the nature of the Internet feel very anonymous in it, which in turn leads to more violations of the image and the need to protect this good and prevent their violations. it requires a certain mechanism, methods to protect personal rights post-mortem on social networks.

It has been noticed before that the Polish legal system mainly uses the construction of the protection of the deceased's personal rights related to the violation of the deceased's cult and memory. This concept indicates that the legitimated entity may use all available means of protection until such application resulting from one regulation is the same or is not excluded by the second measure provided by law. As noted in the first chapter, based on art. 24 k.c., the entity legitimized for the violation of personal good in the form of the cult and memory of the deceased person is entitled to non-property and property claims. It is also worth recalling here. Non-pecuniary ones include: o omission, for the removal of the consequences of the violation and a claim for establishing, and for property: financial compensation or payment of an appropriate sum for a social purpose and repairing property damage in the event that this occurrence[99].

In the case when there has been a violation of the creator's personal good, it is also possible to use, as mentioned in this work, the regulation of copyright law. As a rule, the entities authorized under the provision of art. 78 paragraph 1 p.a. they are entitled to claims for the protection of personal copyrights. It is also important that non-proprietary claims clearly have a fundamental character here. In the case of action that

[99] Z. Lisowska, *Ochrona prawa do wizerunku w Internecie*, w: E. Galewska (red.), *Wybrane aspekty prawa nowych technologii, cz. 3*, Wrocław 2015, s. 167-169.

threatens to violate, the rightholder has the right to demand the abandonment of the action, which of course - simultaneously - is a preventive measure of this protection. In the event of a violation already committed, the legitimated entity may request completion of actions that are necessary to remove the effects. In this case, the declaration on the relevant content and form or an apology deserves special attention[100].

It should also be pointed out that the right holder has an obvious right to make claims also property, and therefore for compensation for the harm suffered or to pay a sum of money for the indicated social purpose. An important and demanding accent is the feature of this claim, which is vested in the claimant only in the event of violation of the culpable. In contrast to art. 448 k.c., art. 78 paragraph 1 p.a. indicates the premise of guilt of the offender as the basis for redress[101]. It is also significant that it is emphasized that the burden of proof rests with the entity that disseminated the image. Judgments of the courts confirm that the person who has violated the image must prove that his action was not unlawful and that the dissemination of the image did not go beyond the specified purpose or the limit of the license[102].

In the case of violation of the personal good of a deceased person on the Internet, especially on social networks, it should be borne in mind that authorized entities may use the provisions contained in the Act on the provision of electronic services. The provisions laid down there indicate that the deceased's family members have the right to refer the request to the service provider for the removal or immediate prevention of access to the indicated materials, which were the cause of the violation. At this point, it should be emphasized that on the basis of art. 13 paragraph 2 and art. 14 of this act, the service provider who stores the data, e.g. the image of the deceased person, is not responsible for their storage, if not their illegitimacy or related activities. In the event that the service provider receives official notification or obtains a credible confirmation of unlawfulness, he is obliged to immediately remove or prevent access to such data[103].

Application of the construction from art. 14 para. 2 and 3 of the Act on the provision of

[100] E. Ferenc - Szydełko, w: E. Ferenc- Szydełko (red.), *Ustawa o prawie autorskim i prawach pokrewnych. Komentarz*, Warszawa 2015, s. 515-548.
[101] T. Grzeszak, *Prawo do bycia...*, s. 714.
[102] J. Barta, R. Markiewicz (red.), *Ustawa...*, dz. cyt., Warszawa 2016, s. 530-532.
[103] Z. Lisowska, *Dobra osobiste...*, s. 46.

electronic services, and thus, disabling access to data, the service provider is released from liability, also for possible damage to the entity that placed the content that is the subject of a notification or a reliable message[104].

In the case of protection of the post-mortem image, the main means of protection is the use of the construction of the cult and memory of the deceased person - in accordance with art. 24 k.c .. Therefore, the rights of the deceased somehow revive as the rights of people who during his life were close to him. They are entitled to request the removal of certain data of the deceased from the Internet, even those that have been placed there by the deceased himself. Of course, each time it will be necessary to assess whether the violation of the personal good of a loved one is unlawful and whether it meets objective criteria[105].

3.3. Problems of post mortem protection on social networks

In addition to the above-mentioned constructions, the practical approach to post-mortem image protection is very interesting, the introduction of memoriam status through social networking sites. This form is reflected in Facebook, which provides the possibility of assigning such status. Can one wonder if it fully avoids the negative consequences of the information stored on the portal? Certainly not, but partly - one can agree - that this is a solution that aims to provide the deceased with the attribute of dignity. An interesting example related to the problem of post mortem image protection is pointed out by Z. Lisowska. The author presented the case of Julianna Ribeiro Campos, a journalist who contacts readers through a social networking site. When she died, her account was still active, although she had no influence on the shape and content that was posted there. Julianna's mother wanted to delete the journalist's account. Therefore, she wrote to the profile administrator.
Initially, it was not possible to effectively block the profile or delete it, but it was blocked for access to the account by people who did not know the deceased, i.e. they were not related to her profile. In the end, the case was settled in Brazil, which in a

[104] X. Konarski, *Komentarz do ustawy o świadczeniu usług drogą elektroniczną*, Warszawa 2014, s. 142.
[105] W. Dubis, M. Daćków, *Prawo do bycia zapomnianym w Internecie - za życia i po śmierci?*, w: *Non omnis moriar...*, dz. cyt., s. 174-187.

decision against Facebook ordered the removal of the account of a deceased journalist. You can easily assume that this was a premise for Facebook to enter the appropriate procedure for the account of the deceased user. You have the option to suspend your account and create a status in memoriam, or completely delete your profile[106].

The most popular social networking site - Facebook - allowed anyone to submit a special application for the account of the deceased user. The form allows reporting of death and removal request, or - as already mentioned - special status setting - in memoriam. Such profile of the deceased user has all interactions excluded and is a kind of commemorative profile[107].

It is worth pointing out that ante mortem can be an account supervisor (through another Facebook form). Then, after the user's death, such a person may change the profile picture or post. For obvious reasons, however, there is no access to all information, can not delete friends, can not send or receive messages of the deceased person. If the guardian is not established, the profile of the deceased user is administered by social network managers. It should also be emphasized that the profile in memoriam will not be able to be searched by people who are not friends of the user[108].

When examining the relations between users and social networks, it should be pointed out that they are a compilation of many legal relationships from many branches of law, which makes this topic extremely wide and complicated. Facebook here and post-mortem mechanisms are certainly a positive aspect of the protection of the deceased's personal rights. Also, one can not forget that after the user's death, rights to the works may be violated.

[106] W. Dubis, M. Daćków, dz. cyt., s. 174-187.
[107] http://www.facebook.com/help, dostęp: 13.05.2017 r.
[108] Z. Lisowska, *Dobra osobiste...*, s. 47.

SUMMARY AND CONCLUSIONS

The right to protect the image is one of the civil rights which is referred to in Chapter II of the Constitution of the Republic of Poland in art. 30 and 47, thus ensuring the protection of the order to respect the rights of others addressed to everyone. Restrictions in the use of constitutional freedoms and civil rights are only allowed in special cases established by law. Legal regulations regarding the image of a person are also indicated in the Civil Code (Articles 23, 24).

One should be very careful and cautious about the issues of publishing the image of a given natural person on the Internet. Once again, it is necessary to emphasize the fact of special protection and the lack of freedom to publish the image, of course, unless there is a statutory limitation of the right to protect the image or - as noted in the work - the publication was allowed. The norms of Polish law also include the protection of legal persons and business entities, which should be subject to similar rules. European Union law provides both types of image with a broader legal protection than national law. This protection also applies to all publications on the Internet.

The author's intention was to show the protection of the image as a personal good in vivo and post mortem of a physical person.

It is noted that personal goods are an attribute of every physical person. The laws that correspond to these things belong to every human being from the moment of conception until death. On the basis of civil law, their protection is implemented by granting subjective rights of absolute, effective erga omnes, non-hereditary and inalienable. Prevailing in the doctrine of this view undoubtedly strengthens this protection because of the presumption of unlawfulness of their violation.

The image is subject to the regulation of the Civil Code and copyright law. And when, in the case of civil law norms, it is about protecting interests: mental and physical integrity of an individual, image, somehow an attribute of this person and the right to present it in a real light, copyright law deals with the protection of property interests related to violation monopoly on the exploitation of one's own image.

It seems that in order to assess what interest was infringed, it would be necessary to use the criteria elaborated by J. Balcarczyk, namely the classical and commercial image, however, they were still the same image. Such generalization of concepts would help avoid excessive casuistry and create new concepts of the image which, as indicated, do not bring anything new in the doctrine. General constructions which concretize ad casu are more effective in American law and correspond to the pace of changing social relations, but at the same time do not cause too complicated institutions.

It should be noted that the work consists of three chapters, devoted respectively to the concept of notion and protection of the image in Polish law, violations of the image on social networks, as well as the situation of post mortem protection.

The first chapter pointed to the subject of legal protection of the image, beginning with the explanation of the concept of image, protection of the image as a personal good and other branches of law.

The second chapter contains the content of the right to the image of users of social networking sites, it was indicated as recognizable as a feature of the legal protection of the image. Next, the attention was focused on the permission to disseminate the image and limit the right to the image, to finally indicate the sanctions and legitimacy active and passive in the case of violations of image protection, and therefore protective claims.

The third chapter deals with the essence of personal rights, ante but above all post mortem. It was pointed out that in the era of the great popularity of the Internet and social networks, such regulations should be created that would serve preventive actions aimed at preventing infringements of personal rights and, if violations occur, enable effective protection of certain goods, especially image, widely discussed in the study. There is no doubt that the protection of the image as a personal good of any natural person should be possible in vivo, let alone strengthened by post mortem. The memory of the dead, as a personal good, includes the honor, dignity, and image of these people. An example of a violation of personal interests may be the illicit use of an image, family name or coat of arms, in particular when the person responsible for such behavior is entitled to financial benefits. This problem is so complicated that it usually requires an interpretation of the ad casum court.

The source materials used in this work reveal not only the fact of the legal protection of the image - the personal good of users of social networking sites, but also indicate the important problems of similar post mortem protection.

It is worth noting that in the matter of protecting the image of the deceased, the use of the protection of the cult and memory of the deceased is still in force - pursuant to art. 24 k.c.- when the rights of the deceased are revived as the rights of persons close to him. And as noted, the protection of personal rights post-mortem can be performed by relatives after the death of a natural person, among others by removing from the portal the data of the deceased, even when he voluntarily placed them there. It is then necessary to assess the actual state of whether an unlawful violation of a personal good has been assessed according to objective criteria.

An adequate level of protection of personal data and image protection is provided, for example, by Canada. Her two regulations regarding the protection of personal data: Personal Information Protection and the Electronic Documents Act. The Canadian Privacy Commissioner has jurisdictions covering "real and significant" activity of a given entity (social networking site) with Canada. This regulation allows the Commissioner to act on behalf of the citizens of his country when their rights are violated on social networks and respond appropriately.

Therefore, it is worth considering in the context of Canadian solutions, should they not be used as a model in European countries. A solution that could guarantee greater legal protection for users of social networking sites in Poland could be the dependence of jurisdiction on whether, for example, a given service is addressed to Polish citizens.

BIBLIOGRAPHY

SOURCE OF LAW:

1. The Constitution of the Republic of Poland of April 2, 1997,
(Journal of Laws No. 78, item 483, as amended Journal of Laws No. 117, item 557, as amended).
2. The Act of 23 April 1964 - the Civil Code (ie, Journal of Laws of 2016, item 380).
3. The Act of November 17, 1964 - Code of Civil Procedure
(volume, No. 2016, No. 0, item 1822).
4. The Act of August 29, 1997 on the Protection of Personal Data
(ie, Journal of Laws of 2016, item 922)
5. The Act of February 4, 1994 on copyright and related rights
(ie OJ of 2017, item 880)
6. The Act of 30 June 2000 - Industrial Property Law
(ie OJ 2017, No. 0, item 776)

LITERATURE:

Balcarczyk J. (red.), Personal goods in the 21st century, Warsaw 2012.
Balcarczyk J., Is it allowed to call in association with a specific person ?, in: M. Namysłowska (ed.), Reklama. Legal aspects, Warsaw 2012
Balcarczyk J., The right to image and its commercialization, Oficyna 2009, Lex No. 94267.
Barta J. (ed.), Markiewicz R. (ed.), Czajkowska-Dąbrowska M., Ćwiąkalski Z., Felchner K., Traple E., Law on copyright and related rights. Commentary, Warsaw 2011, LEX No. 94267.
Barta J. (ed.), Copyright law. Private Law System. Tom 13, Warsaw 2017.

Barta J., Fajgielski P., Markiewicz R., art. 6, in: Barta J., Fajgielski P., Markiewicz R., Protection of personal data. Commentary, Warsaw 2011, Lex No. 106637.

Barta J., Markiewicz R., Copyright, Warsaw 2013.

Barta J., The right to the image and the right of the addressee of correspondence, in: Copyright Law, System of Private Law Volume 13, ed. 4, Warsaw 2017.

Błeszyński J., Prawo copyright, Warsaw 1988.

10. Brzozowska M., Violation of personal rights on the Internet on Internet forums, MoP 2014, No. 2.

Dmowski S., Rudnicki S., Commentary to the Civil Code. Book one. General part, Warsaw 2015.

Fajgielski P. (red.), Protection of personal data in Poland from the perspective of the decade, Lublin 2008.

Ferenc-Szydełko E. (ed.), Law on copyright and related rights. Commentary, Warsaw 2015.

Gniewek E. (ed.), Fundamentals of civil law, Warsaw 2011.

Gniewek E., Machnikowski P., Civil Code. Commentary, Warsaw 2016.

Gołaczyński J., Mazurkiewicz J., Turłukowski J., Karkut D., Non omnis moriar. Personal and property legal aspects of human death. Selected issues, Wrocław 2015.

Goździaszek Ł., Liquidation of identity on a social website, pp. 298-310. Goździaszek Ł., Blogosphere Law, Warsaw 2014.

Grzybczyk K., Breach of personal good in advertising, "Rejent" 1999, No. 9.

Grzybowski S., Protection of personal rights according to general civil law, Warsaw 1957.

Konarski X., Commentary to the Act on electronic services, Warsaw 2014.

Lisowska Z., Personal goods of the deceased and the possibility of their protection on the Internet, PME 2016 No. 2.

Lisowska Z., Protection of the right to image on the Internet, in: E. Galewska (ed.), Selected aspects of the law of new technologies, part 2 3, Wrocław 2015.

Lucas-Schlotter A., in: A. Ohly, H. Beverly-Smith, A. Lucas - Schlotter, Privacy, Property and Personality - Civil Law Pespectives on Commercial Appropriation, Cambridge 2005.

Majos M., Protection of image and personal data on social networks, in: Starik N. (ed.), Zduniak A. (ed.), Subjectivity in education versus cultural differences and social differentiations. Education of the 21st century (vol. 1/27), Poznań 2013, pp. 159-171.

Marciniak G., Cyberbullying: threats related to the use of modern information technologies, in: V. Tanaś (ed.), W. Welskop (ed.), Education in a globalized world, Łódź 2016, pp. 325-336.

Marciniak G., Orliński K., Leisure as an individual right - a phenomenon of free time, in: V. Tanaś (ed.), W. Welskop (ed.), Culture of free time in the modern world, Łódź 2016, p. 349-359.

Matlak A., Civil Law Protection of the Image, KPP 2004, z. 2.

Pazdan M., in: Civil Code. Commentary on Articles 1-449, K. Pietrzykowski (ed.), Warsaw 2016.

Radwański Z. (red.), Green Book. Optimal vision of the Civil Code in the Republic of Poland, Warsaw 2006.

Radwański Z., Olejniczak A., Civil law - general part, Warsaw 2011.

Radwański Z., Civil law - general part, Warsaw 1997.

Ritterman S., Commentary on the Copyright Act, Kraków 1937.

Safjan M. (ed.), Civil law - general part. Private Law System. Volume 1, Warsaw 2012.

Sieńczyło-Chlabicz J., Subject, subject and character of the right to the image, PUG 2003, No.

Sołtysiński S., Legal character of the inventor, Poznań 1967.

Stefaniuk K., Violation of the right of image by the dissemination of a likeness, PiP 1970 nr 1.

Szpor G., The concept of information and the scope of personal data, in: Fajgielski P. (ed.), Protection of personal data in Poland from the perspective of the decade, Lublin 2008.

Tomczyk M., Foto-clubbing: legal aspects, „ Humanist Education "No. 1 (26) 2012, Szczecin 2012, pp. 171-179.

Traple E., Personal goods in advertising, in: The law of advertising and promotion, ed. E. Traple, Warsaw 2007.

Wilejczyk M., Ethical issues of the general part of civil law, Warsaw 2014.

JURISPRUDENCE:

1. Decision of the Grand Chamber of the ECtHR of 16/06/2015, in the case of Delfi AS v. Estonia 64596/09.
2. Judgment of the Supreme Court of 19 September 1968, II CR 291/68, OSNCP 1969/11/200.
3. Judgment of the Supreme Court of 18 January 1984, I CR 400/83, OSN 1984, item 195.
4. Judgment of the SA of April 11, 2001, Ref. Act I ACa 244.01, TPP 2002, No. 3.
5. Judgment of the SA in Kraków of 19 December 2001, Ref. Act I ACa 957/01, TPP 2002, No. 3, p. 108.
6. Judgment of the SA of June 20, 2002, Ref. Act I ACa 1358.01.
7. Judgment of the Supreme Court of 27 February 2003, Ref. act IV CKN 1819/00.
8. Judgment of the SA in Warsaw of November 26, 2003, Ref. act VI ACa 384/03, unpublished
9. Judgment of the Supreme Court dated 20.05.2004, reference number Act II CK 330/03, Biul. SN 2004, No. 11.
10. Judgment of the SA in Warsaw of 19.04.2000, reference number file: I ACa 1455/99, Legalis.
11. Judgment of the SA in Warsaw of 10 February 2005, Ref. Act I ACa 509/04, unpublished
12. Judgment of the Supreme Court of 20 May 2005, Ref. Act II CK 330/03, Bulletin SN 2004 No. 11.
13. Judgment of the SA in Warsaw of October 27, 2005, Ref. Act VI ACa 838.04. Legalis.
14. Judgment of the Company in Wrocław of 26 February 2007, Ref. Act I ACa 1492/06, OSA 2007, No. 3, item 41.
15. Judgment of the Supreme Court of 20 July 2007, Ref. act I CSK 134.07, Legalis.
16. Judgment of the Supreme Court of 5 November 2008, Ref. act I CSK 164/08, Legalis.

17. Judgment of the Supreme Court of 15 October 2009, Ref. I CSK 72/09, OSNC 2010 No. 1, item 29.
18. The judgment of the Supreme Administrative Court in Warsaw of 19.05.2011, Ref. I OSK 1079/10.
19. Judgment of the SA in Warsaw of 3 December. 2010, reference number VI ACa 725/10, unpublished
20. Judgment of the SA in Białystok of November 14, 2012, reference number Act I ACa 543/12, Legalis.
21. Judgment of the SA in Warsaw of 7 May 2014, Ref. Act I ACa 1686/13, Legalis.
22. Judgment of the SA of February 24, 2016, Ref. Act. I ACa 1630/15, Legalis.

MIX
Papier aus verantwortungsvollen Quellen
Paper from responsible sources
FSC® C105338

Printed by Books on Demand GmbH, Norderstedt / Germany